Baby Quilts

Baby Quilts

Original Designs
for Every Nursery Décor

EDITED BY LINDA NEUBAUER

APPLE

First published in the UK by Apple Press
4th Floor
Sheridan House
114 Western Road
Hove BN3 1DD
www.apple-press.com

Created and produced by Creative Publishing international
18705 Lake Drive East
Chanhassen, MN 55317
U.S.A.
www.creativepub.com

ISBN 1-84543-113-8

Printed in China

10 9 8 7 6 5 4 3 2 1

Contents

Sewing Baby Quilts

What more thoughtful gift could you make for a newborn than a cuddly baby quilt? With loving attention to every stitch, a quilt shares your creative talent, provides warmth and comfort, and becomes a treasured keepsake for the child.

We wanted the projects in this book to represent a variety of styles and quilting techniques, so we asked for projects from five talented designers and gave each of them different guidelines. Gerri Robinson designed three quilts that feature very textured fabrics and unexpected surface effects. Susan Stein's quilts are block-pieced in unique ways with vibrant, contemporary colors. Sharon Hultgren developed three foundation-pieced quilt patterns, each with a very distinctive look. Janis Bullis provided us with three cuddly appliquéd baby quilts. Phyllis Dobbs designed quick-and-easy quilts with large center panels, big blocks, and wide borders. There is sure to be a project to suit every quilter and every baby.

Each project has a complete materials list, cutting instructions, and step-by-step directions for sewing the quilt tops. How you quilt and bind the quilts is usually a matter of personal preference, though special instructions are provided for some of the projects. The materials lists include the fabrics and notions you need to buy but don't include the things you probably have on hand, such as measuring and cutting tools, marking pens, quilter's safety pins, and sewing thread. All seam allowances are ¼" (6 mm) wide and are included in the cutting directions and templates.

You can copy the designs closely or choose different fabrics and colors to suit the nursery décor or the preferences of the parents. With the fifteen designs in this book and a world of quilting fabrics to choose from, the possibilities for baby quilts are unlimited. Pick your favorite and let the quilting begin!

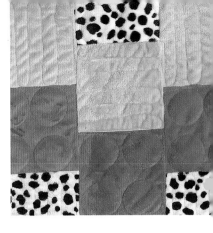

Super Plush

Minkee block quilt

If you have never touched the wonderful Minkee fabrics by Benartex, you are in for a real treat. They are so plush and soothing, you can't stop yourself from "petting" them. Just imagine how gentle and comforting they would be in a baby quilt!

Minkee fabrics are now widely available in quilt shops and other fabric stores, and people are looking for new ways to use them. To make the most of the texture, this quilt is made up of simple blocks. I chose bright colors and Dalmatian spots. You can opt for the pastel colors, if you prefer. Because of the natural thickness and body of Minkee fabrics, batting isn't necessary in this quilt.

Gerri Robinson

FINISHED SIZE: 48" × 58" (122 × 147 cm)

TECHNIQUES USED: Quilting with textured fabric, mitered-corner binding

Cutting Directions

One 6½" (16.3 cm) full crosswise strip of each Blankee color; cut seven 6½" (16.3 cm) squares from each strip

Three 6½" (16.3 cm) full crosswise strips of Dalmatian; cut 14 6½" (16.3 cm) squares from two strips; cut seven 3½" × 6½" (9 × 16.3 cm) rectangles from the third strip

Four 3½" (9 cm) full crosswise strips of Dalmatian for borders

Four 3½" (9 cm) full crosswise strips of binding fabric

Materials

- ¼ yd. (0.25 m) each of six colors of Benartex Minkee Blankee fabric: purple, orange, yellow, fuchsia, royal blue, green
- 1 yd. (0.92 m) Dalmatian Minkee Skin
- 1⅞ yd. (1.75 m) Minkee fabric of choice for backing
- ½ yd. (0.5 m) Minkee fabric of choice for binding

Designer's Tip

To sew on Minkee fabrics, use a universal needle, size 80/12. Attach a walking foot to your machine to help the layers feed evenly. If pressing is necessary, set the iron on medium setting and press lightly to avoid stretching the fabric.

3

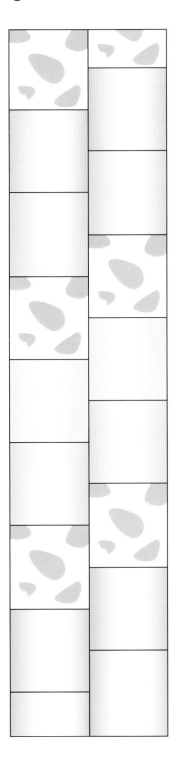

1. Arrange the pieces in order on a design wall or work surface, using the photograph on page 8 as a guide.

2. Stitch the pieces of each column together. Lightly press the seam allowances open.

3. Stitch the columns together, matching the seams in one column to the centers of the squares in the next column.

4. Measure the quilt top to bottom through the center. Cut two border strips to this length. Sew the borders to the sides of the quilt. Press the seam allowances toward the borders.

5. Measure the quilt side to side through the center, including the side borders. Cut two border strips to this length. Sew the borders to the top and bottom of the quilt. Press the seam allowances toward the borders.

6. Cut the backing to the same size as the quilt top. Place the backing and quilt top wrong sides together. Machine-baste ¼" (6 mm) from the outer edges. Baste the layers together with safety pins placed about 6" (15 cm) apart.

7. Quilt by machine. The quilt on page 8 was quilted free-motion in alternating rows of circles and lines. Following the diagram, you can stitch from one side of the quilt to the other without stopping.

8. Join the binding strips with diagonal seams; press the seams open. Bind the quilt, using the continuous method and mitering the corners as on page 28, steps 16 to 18. Stitch ½" (1.3 cm) from the edge instead of the usual ⅜" (1 cm) to allow for the extra bulk of the fabric.

7

8

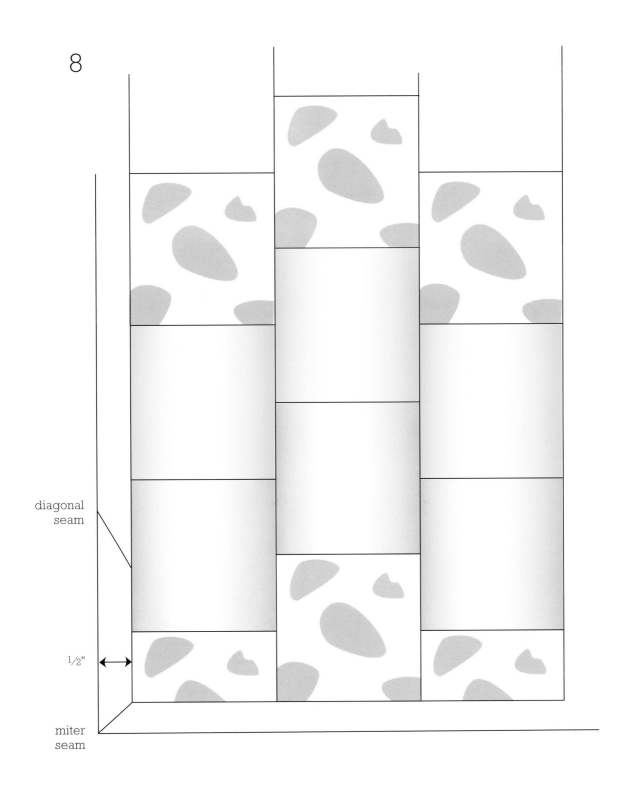

diagonal
seam

1/2"

miter
seam

Soft Touch

Flannel block quilt

Flannel fabrics, with their softness and warmth, make cuddly quilts for babies. For this bold block quilt, I used a collection of brightly colored flannels that have a printed background for visual texture, too. Large blocks and four-patch blocks are arranged randomly throughout the quilt to create an interesting collage of color. Choose a variety of light and medium values in both warm and cool colors to achieve this look.

Gerri Robinson

Finished Size: 46" × 52" (117 × 132 cm)

Techniques Used: Simple block piecing

Cutting Directions

Twenty-eight 6½" (16.3 cm) squares of brightly colored flannels

Three 3½" (9 cm) crosswise strips each of the warm and cool colors for the four-patch blocks

One 5" (12.7 cm) full crosswise strip of each fabric for top and bottom borders

Two 5" (12.7 cm) full crosswise strips of each fabric for side borders

Materials

- One fat quarter each of eight different flannel fabrics for large blocks
- One fat quarter each of four different brightly colored flannels for four-patch blocks (two warm and two cool colors)
- ¼ yd. (0.25 m) each of two flannels for top and bottom borders
- ⅓ yd. (0.32 m) each of two flannels for side borders
- ½ yd. (0.5 m) flannel for binding
- 3 yd. (2.75 m) flannel for backing
- One low-loft crib batting

1. Sew a cool strip to a warm strip lengthwise, joining three sets of the same color combination. Press the seam allowances toward the cool strips. Cut the strips into 14 units 3½" (9 cm) wide. These will be called unit 1.

2. Sew the other cool strips to the other warm strips lengthwise, joining three sets of the same color combination. Press the seam allowances toward the cool strips. Cut the strips into 14 units 3½" (9 cm) wide. These will be called unit 2.

1

6½"

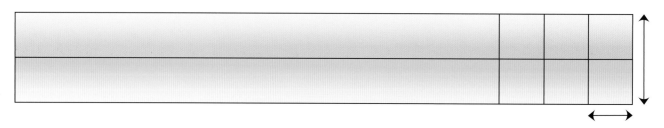

3½"

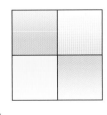

3

3. Sew each unit 1 to a unit 2 to create 14 four-patch blocks. Press the seam allowances toward 2.

4. Arrange the four-patch blocks and the 6½" (16.3 cm) blocks on a design wall or work surface, following the photograph on page 14. Sew the blocks together in rows.

5. Sew the rows together, aligning seams.

6. Measure the quilt side to side through the center. Cut border strips to this length. Sew one to the top and one to the bottom of the quilt. Press the seam allowances toward the borders.

7. Measure the quilt top to bottom through the center, including the top and bottom borders. Piece two border strips together, press the seam allowances open, and cut the border to this length. Repeat for the other side border. Sew one border to each side of the quilt. Press the seam allowances toward the borders.

8. Press the quilt top. Piece the backing. Cut the backing and batting slightly larger than the quilt top. Layer the backing, batting, and quilt top; baste with safety pins or by hand.

9. Quilt as desired. If you prefer to see your thread on your quilt, use a heavier quilting thread. The lighter threads will sink down into the flannel fibers.

10. Bind the quilt as desired.

Designer's Tip

I do not prewash or preshrink any of my fabric. When the quilt is completely finished, I toss it in a gentle wash and a tumble dry cycle so all the fabrics and batting will shrink together. I love the soft, rumpled look. I do use a fabric dye sheet, such as Shout Color Catcher, in the wash cycle to catch any excess color that may bleed. This has always worked for me and no quilt has ever been ruined.

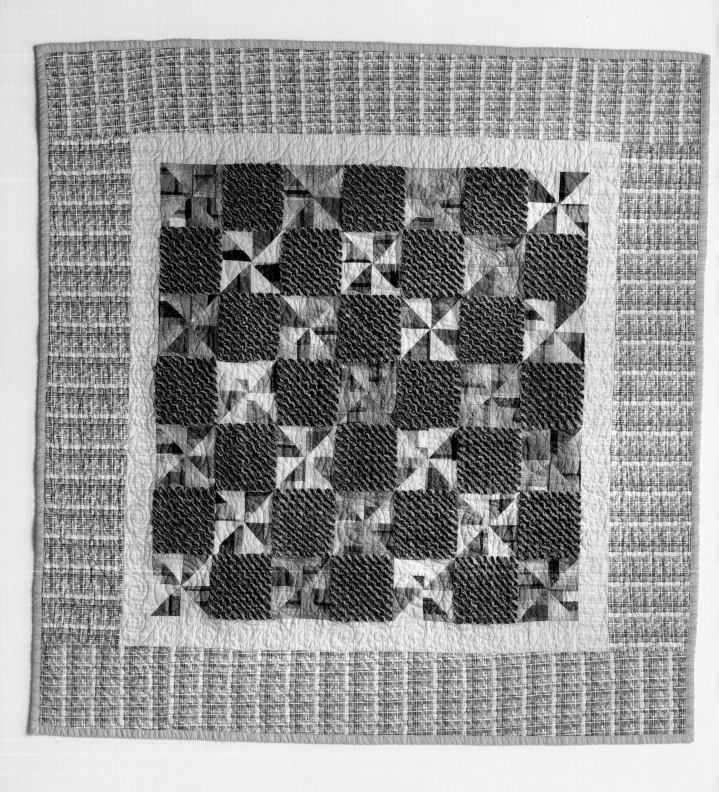

Warm Fuzzies

Chenille and pinwheels quilt

This quilt is fun to look at and just as much fun to touch! Babies love to explore with their fingers new textures like the rumpled ridges of the faux chenille squares in this quilt. Layers of fabrics are sewn together in bias channels and then the top layers are slashed. When the quilt is washed the first time, the slashed edges fluff up to create the look of chenille.

Experiment with the fabrics for your chenille squares. Fabrics that have color on both sides work the best, and you'll need five layers. Sometimes just changing the order of the fabrics makes a big difference.

Gerri Robinson

FINISHED SIZE: 44" × 44" (112 × 112 cm)

TECHNIQUES USED: Faux chenille, pinwheel blocks

Materials

- ¼ yd. (0.25 m) each of five fabrics for pinwheels: pink, yellow, lime green, turquoise, and multi
- 1 yd. (0.92 m) each of five fabrics for chenille squares: multi, yellow, turquoise/black, pink, green/turquoise
- ⅓ yd. (0.32 m) yellow fabric for inner border
- ¾ yd. (0.7 m) plaid fabric for outer border
- 1⅜ yd. (1.3 m) fabric, 45" (115 cm) wide or 2¾ yd. (2.55 m) if narrower, for backing
- One low-loft crib batting
- ⅜ yd. (0.35 m) lime green fabric for binding
- Clover Slash Cutter or sharp embroidery scissors

Cutting Directions

One 2⅞" (7.2 cm) full crosswise strip of pink; cut into 14 squares, each cut in half diagonally to yield 28 triangles for pinwheels

One 2⅞" (7.2 cm) full crosswise strip of yellow, lime green, and turquoise; cut 12 squares from each strip then cut each in half diagonally to yield 24 triangles of each color for pinwheels

Four 2⅞" (7.2 cm) full crosswise strips of multicolor fabric; cut into 50 squares; then cut each in half diagonally to yield 100 triangles for pinwheels

Three 15" (38 cm) squares from each of the five fabrics for chenille blocks

Four 2½" (6.5 cm) full crosswise strips of fabric for inner border

Four 6" (15 cm) full crosswise strips of fabric for outer border

Four 2½" (6.5 cm) full crosswise strips of binding fabric

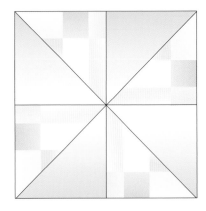

3

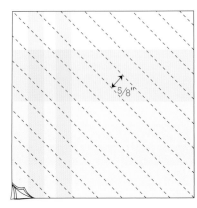

5/8"

5

1. Place a multicolor triangle and a solid color triangle right sides together. Stitch together on the long, bias edge, taking care not to stretch the seam.

2. Press the seam allowances toward the multicolored fabric. Trim off the "dog ears."

3. Repeat steps 1 and 2 for all the triangles to make 100 triangle squares. Sew them together in matching sets of four to make 25 pinwheel blocks with a finished size of 4½" (11.5 cm) square.

4. Layer the 15" (38 cm) squares of fabric, right sides up, in order from bottom to top: multicolor, yellow, turquoise/black, pink, green/turquoise. You will have three sets of five fabrics each. Pin the layers together, inserting the pins in diagonal rows.

5. Sew the layers together in a diagonal line from corner to corner. Reverse the direction and sew another line ⅝" (1.5 cm) from the first one. Continue sewing lines ⅝" (1.5 cm) apart, reversing the direction, until you reach the outer corner. Then sew lines on the opposite side of the center. Repeat for each set of layered squares.

Designer's Tip

A Clover Slash Cutter is designed specifically for making faux chenille. It has a narrow guide that slides into the channel just above the foundation layer and a small rotary cutter that slashes the upper layers. Small, sharp embroidery scissors also work well for slashing the fabrics. Take care not to cut the bottom layer.

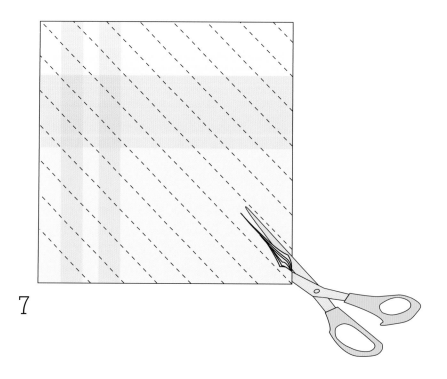

7

8

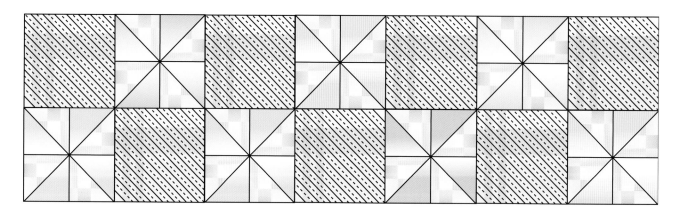

6. Cut each channel-stitched square into nine 4½" (11.5 cm) squares. You will need 24 squares for the quilt.

7. Slash the top four layers of fabric halfway between the stitching lines in each channel for each of the squares.

8. Arrange the blocks of the quilt top in seven rows, alternating pinwheel blocks and chenille blocks in each row and column. Arrange the colors of the pinwheels randomly. Keep all the diagonal lines of the chenille squares running in the same direction.

9. Sew the blocks together for each row. Then sew the rows together.

10. Measure the quilt top to bottom through the center. Cut two inner border strips to this length. Sew the inner borders to the sides of the quilt. Press the seam allowances toward the borders.

11. Measure the quilt side to side through the center, including the side borders. Cut two inner border strips to this length. Sew the inner borders to the top and bottom of the quilt.

12. Attach the outer border, following the procedure in steps 10 and 11.

13. Cut batting and backing slightly larger than the quilt top. Layer the backing, batting, and quilt top; baste with safety pins or by hand. Quilt by machine. Do not quilt in the chenille squares.

14. Bind the quilt.

15. Wash the quilt in the machine in mild soap and cool water with moderate agitation. Dry the quilt in the dryer. The chenille squares will fluff nicely.

Sail Off to Sleep

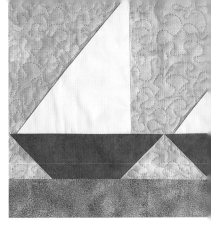

Paper-pieced block quilt

£iving on a lake in northern Minnesota, I spend much of my free time relaxing on the shore and watching the water. On breezy mornings, the sailboats often venture out to take advantage of nature's power and glide quietly across the waves. Small children, particularly little boys, love boats, so it seemed like a fitting subject for a baby quilt. The sailboat, with its geometric lines, was easy to design as a foundation-pieced pattern. The blocks can be sewn together quickly. You can follow my color scheme or choose several colors for the boat bodies.

Sharon Hultgren

FINISHED SIZE: 40" × 49" (102 × 125 cm)

TECHNIQUES USED: Foundation piecing, stipple quilting or method of choice, mitered-corner binding

Cutting Directions

Light blue sky fabric; cut into smaller pieces at least ½"
(1.3 cm) larger than each of the four sky areas in the block
(16 of each piece)

Eight 9" (23 cm) squares of white fabric, cut in half diagonally

Sixteen 3" × 8" (7.5 × 20.5 cm) rectangles of red fabric

Three 2½" (6.5 cm) full crosswise strips of medium blue
for water

Four 2" (5 cm) full crosswise strips of yellow fabric for inner
borders

Four 1½" (3.8 cm) full crosswise strips of red fabric for
middle borders

Four 3½" (9 cm) full crosswise strips of medium blue fabric
for outer borders

Four or five 2½" (6.5 cm) full crosswise strips of medium blue
fabric for binding

Materials

- Foundation-piecing paper
- ½ yd. (0.5 m) white fabric
  for sails
- ⅔ yd. (0.63 m) red fabric
  for boats and middle borders
- 1 yd. (0.92 m) light blue
  fabric for sky
- ⅓ yd. (0.32 m) yellow
  fabric for inner border
- 1 yd. (0.92 m) medium
  blue fabric for water, outer
  border, and binding
- 1¼ yd. (1.15 m) fabric for
  backing
- One low-loft crib batting

1. Trace or copy the pattern (page 29) onto foundation-piecing
    paper. Trace the pattern eight times; trace the mirror image
    of the pattern eight times.

2. Place a piece of blue sky fabric, right side up, on
    the blank side of the pattern, over area #1; pin. Fold
    the fabric and pattern on the sewing line between #1
    and #2. This will help you set the second piece in
    place.

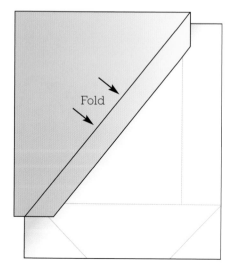

Fold

2

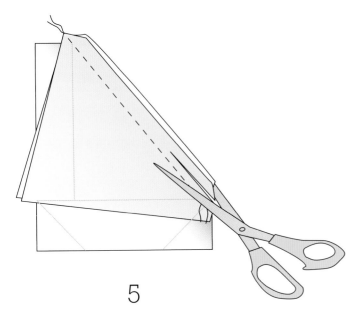

5

3. Place a white triangle over the blue, right sides together; pin along the sewing line. Flip the white fabric over to be sure it will cover area #2; adjust if necessary. Flip the white fabric back in place.

4. From the printed side of the pattern, stitch on the line between areas #1 and #2. Use a short stitch length and stitch a few stitches beyond the ends of the line.

5. With the block printed side up, turn the pattern back on the stitching line and trim the seam allowances to ¼" (6 mm).

6. Fold the pattern back in place. Turn the white fabric over area #2; pin.

7. Apply the fabric for area #3, following steps 3 to 6. Continue until all the areas have been applied.

8. Press the block. Trim away the excess fabric, leaving a ¼" (6 mm) seam allowance beyond the outer pattern line. Carefully tear away the paper pattern.

9. Repeat steps 2 to 8 for all the boat blocks. Sew the boats into four rows of four boats each, with boats in each row facing the same direction. Press the seam allowances open.

10. Measure the rows. Cut all the water strips the same length as the shortest row. Sew the boats and water strips together, alternating the direction of the boats with each row. Match the ends of the strips to the ends of the rows and ease in any excess length. Make sure the blocks align vertically.

11. Measure the quilt top to bottom through the center. Cut two yellow strips to this length. Sew these inner border pieces to the sides of the quilt. Press the seam allowances toward the border.

Designer's Tip

There are several special papers made for foundation piecing. There is even paper that can be dissolved in water after the quilt is sewn! If you use a copy machine to copy the pattern from the book, check the pattern to be sure it has not changed in size. If you copy the pattern by hand, use a pencil, never a ballpoint pen, as the ink can transfer to your fabric.

12. Measure the quilt side to side through the center, including the side inner borders. Cut two yellow strips to this length. Sew the inner border pieces to the top and bottom of the quilt. Press the seam allowances toward the border.

13. Attach the red middle border, following the procedure in steps 11 and 12. Repeat for the outer blue border.

14. Press the quilt. Cut batting and backing slightly larger than the quilt top. Layer the backing, batting, and quilt top; baste with safety pins or by hand. Quilt by machine, outlining the blocks and borders and stipple-quilting the sky. Or use your quilting method of choice.

15. Join the binding strips with ¼" (6 mm) diagonal seams to minimize bulk; press the seam allowances open. Press the binding in half lengthwise, wrong sides together.

16. Stitch the binding to the quilt front, stitching ⅜" (1 cm) from the edge; begin on one side about 3" (7.5 cm) from the end of the binding. At each corner, stop stitching at the exact center of the corner; backstitch two stitches. Fold the binding back diagonally, and then fold it down along the next edge. Start stitching again at the center of the corner, and continue.

17

17. Stop about 3" (7.5 cm) from the starting point. Mark dots on the inside of the binding fold where the beginning and end would meet. Unfold the binding. Place the beginning and end right sides together, perpendicular to each other, aligning the dots. Stitch diagonally across the strips. Trim the seam allowances to ¼" (6 mm) and press open. Refold the binding and finish stitching it in place.

18. Wrap the binding to the back of the quilt, just covering the stitching line with the binding fold and mitering the corners. Stitch in the ditch from the right side.

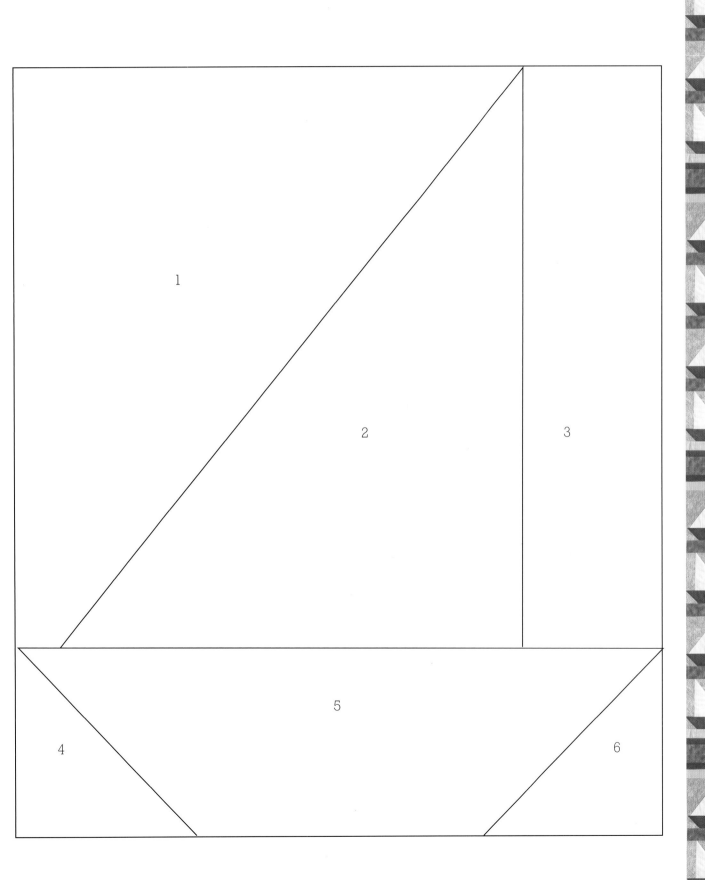

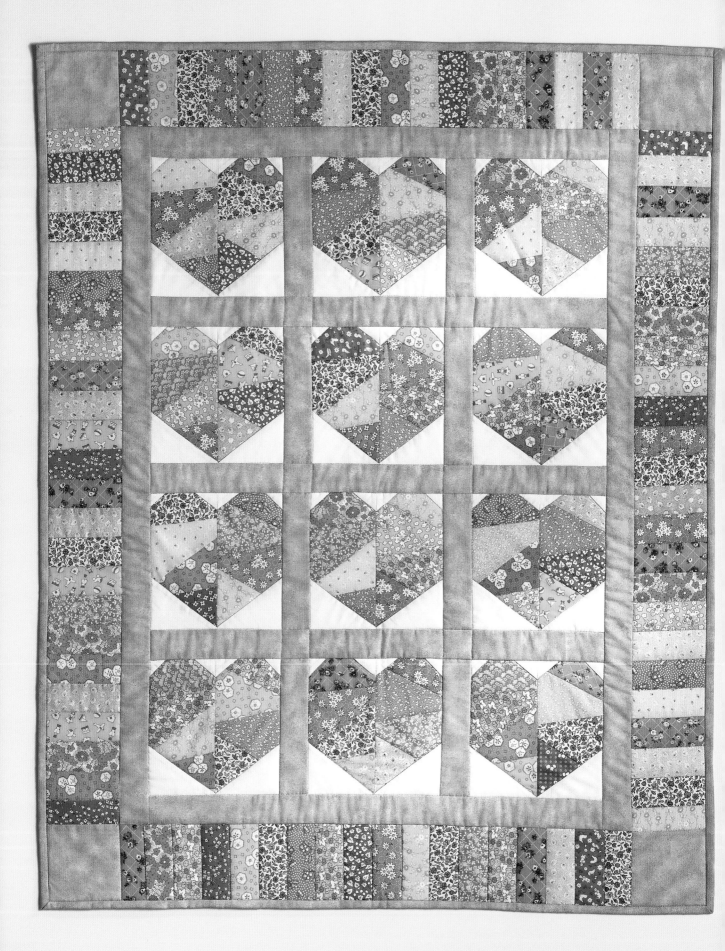

Little Sweetheart

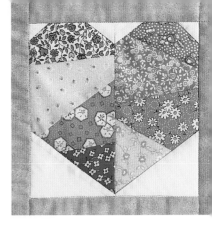

Paper-pieced block quilt

R etro-print pastel fabrics are so sweet and sentimental. I just can't get enough of them, so I was able to pull quite a few from my stash to use in this quilt (I think there are about twenty!). If you don't have a stash like mine to pull from, buy a minimum of eight different fabrics in assorted colors for the pieced hearts. By alternating the fabrics for each area and shuffling them around, you can create twelve unique hearts. The color of the sashing, inner borders, and corner squares can easily be changed to blue for a baby boy or to any other color to match the nursery.

Sharon Hultgren

FINISHED SIZE: 35" × 43½" (89 × 110.3 cm)

TECHNIQUES USED: Foundation piecing, piano key border, mitered-corner binding

Materials

- Foundation-piecing paper
- Eight to 12 fat quarters 18" × 22" (46 × 56 cm) of assorted pastel retro-print fabrics
- ½ yd. (0.5 m) cream fabric for background
- 1 yd. (0.92 m) fabric for sashing, inner border, and binding
- 1½ yd. (1.4 m) fabric for backing
- One low-loft crib batting

Cutting Directions

12 pastel print pieces at least ½" (1.3 cm) larger than each of the eight heart areas in the blocks; alternate fabrics so the same print is not repeated in each heart

Twelve 5" (12.7 cm) squares of cream background fabric; cut in half diagonally

Twenty-four 2½" (6.5 cm) squares of cream background fabric; cut in half diagonally

Nine 2" (5 cm) full crosswise strips of sashing/inner border fabric; cut two of the strips into eight 7½" (19.3 cm) pieces

Eighty-eight 2" × 4½" (5 × 11.5 cm) assorted pastel print rectangles for piano key border

Four 4½" (11.5 cm) squares of sashing/inner border fabric

Four 2½" (6.5 cm) full crosswise strips of binding fabric

1. Trace or copy the patterns (page 34) onto foundation-piecing paper. You will need twelve of each pattern.

2. Arrange the pieces for each heart half in the order in which they will be sewn.

3. Place the fabric piece for area #1, right side up, on the blank side of the pattern, over area #1; pin. Fold the fabric and pattern on the sewing line between #1 and #2. This will help you set the second piece in place.

4. Place the fabric piece for area #2 over the first fabric, right sides together; pin along the sewing line. Flip the second fabric over to be sure it will cover area #2; adjust if necessary. Flip the second fabric back in place.

5. From the printed side of the pattern, stitch on the line between areas #1 and #2. Use a short stitch length and stitch a few stitches beyond the ends of the line.

6. With the block printed side up, turn the pattern back on the stitching line and trim the seam allowances to ¼" (6 mm).

7. Fold the pattern back in place. Turn the second fabric over area #2; pin.

8. Apply the fabric for area #3, following steps 4 to 7. Continue until all the areas have been applied.

9. Press the block. Trim away the excess fabric, leaving a ¼" (6 mm) seam allowance beyond the outer pattern line.

10

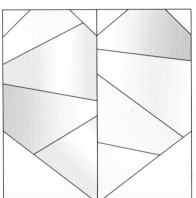

10. Repeat steps 3 to 9 for all the heart halves. Then sew the halves together to make 12 hearts. Carefully tear away the paper pattern. Press the center seam allowances apart.

11. Arrange the hearts in four rows of three hearts each. Join the hearts in each row by stitching a short sashing strip between them. Press the seam allowances toward the sashing strips.

Designer's Tip

Tear away the paper one area at a time, working from the last area sewn to the first. Crease the paper along each seam and then gently tear along the sewn, perforated edge.

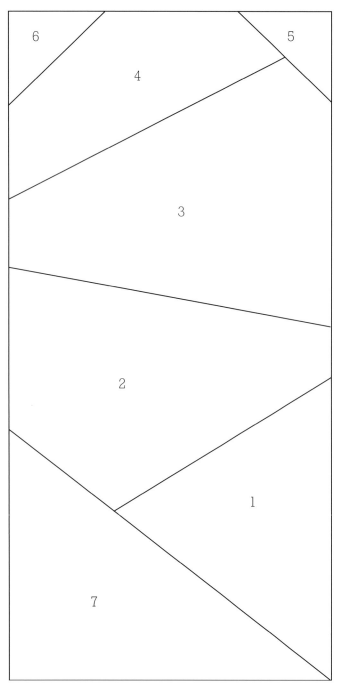
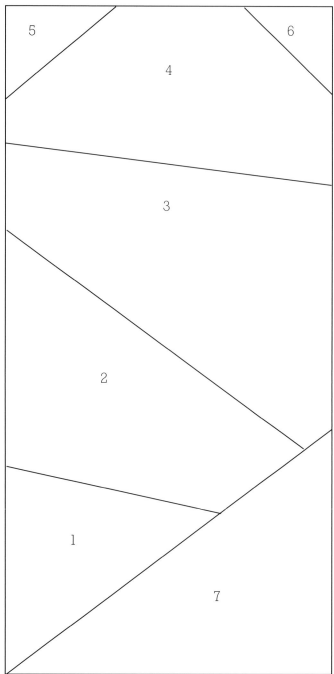

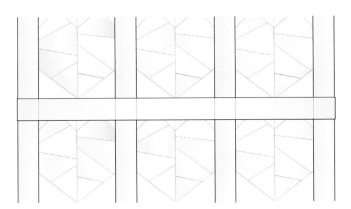

12. Measure the width of the heart rows. Cut five of the long sashing strips to the measurement of the shortest row. Join the rows by stitching sashing strips between the rows; add a sashing strip to the top and bottom. Match the ends of the strips to the ends of the rows and ease in any excess length. Make sure the blocks align vertically.

13. Measure the quilt top to bottom through the center. Cut two inner border strips to this length. Sew the inner borders to the sides of the quilt. Press the seam allowances toward the border.

14. Sew the "piano keys" together, using ¼" (6 mm) seams and alternating fabrics. You will need 24 keys for each side border and 18 keys for the top and bottom borders. Check to see that the borders fit; trim the last keys slightly if necessary.

15. Mark the centers of the quilt sides. Mark the centers of the side borders. Pin the borders to the sides, matching centers and ends. Stitch in place; press the seam allowances toward the inner border.

16. Stitch the squares to the ends of the top and bottom borders; press the seam allowances toward the squares. Stitch the top and bottom borders in place, aligning the corners of the squares to the corners of the inner borders. Press the seam allowances toward the inner borders.

17. Press the quilt. Cut batting and backing slightly larger than the quilt top. Layer the backing, batting, and quilt top; baste with safety pins or by hand. Quilt by machine, outlining the blocks and borders.

18. Bind the quilt following steps 15 to 18 on page 28.

Diamonds Bright

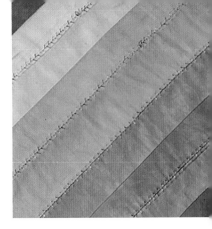

String-pieced block quilt

Babies love colors as much as quilters do. This quilt is sure to make any baby happy, boy or girl. The blocks of diagonal stripes are sewn by string piecing on a foundation. The hand-dyed fabrics that I used are slightly muted with a subtle sueded look that invites you to touch them. When the blocks are arranged and sewn together, they create a dynamic diamond design. Decorative stitching with variegated thread creates a little surface texture. The result is a nice mixture of traditional piecing and contemporary use of color. This is a quilt that can grow up with the child and later become a wall hanging or a décor accent.

Sharon Hultgren

FINISHED SIZE: 43" × 43" (109 × 109 cm)

TECHNIQUES USED: String piecing on a foundation, quilting with decorative machine stitches

Cutting Directions

Six 2¼" (6 cm) full-width strips of medium green fabric; cut into three equal pieces for centers of blocks

Ten 1¾" (4.5 cm) crosswise strips from each of the six fat quarters for blocks

Eight 3" (7.5 cm) squares of red; cut in half diagonally to yield 16 triangles

Eight 3" (7.5 cm) squares of blue; cut in half diagonally to yield 16 triangles

Four 1½" (3.8 cm) full crosswise strips of yellow for accent border

Four 3" (7.5 cm) full crosswise strips of red for first border

Four 3" (7.5 cm) full crosswise strips of blue for second border

Four 3" (7.5 cm) full crosswise strips of green for outer border

Four 2½" (6.5 cm) full crosswise strips of blue binding

Materials

- Foundation-piecing paper
- Six fat quarters 18" × 22" (46 × 56 cm) in assorted hand-dyed colors
- ½ yd. (0.5 m) rosy red fabric for first border
- ¾ yd. (0.7 m) bluebird blue fabric for second border and binding
- ½ yd. (0.5 m) medium green fabric for center strip of block and outer border
- ¼ yd. (0.25 m) yellow fabric for narrow accent border
- 1⅓ yd. (1.23 m) fabric for backing
- One low-loft crib batting
- Variegated thread

1. Trace or copy the pattern (page 41) 16 times onto foundation-piecing paper.

2. Place a green fabric strip, right side up, on the blank side of the pattern, over area #1; pin. Fold the fabric and pattern on the sewing line between #1 and #2. This will help you set the second piece in place.

3. Place a fabric strip for area #2 over the first fabric, right sides together; pin along the sewing line. Flip the second fabric over to be sure it will cover area #2; adjust if necessary. Flip the second fabric back in place.

4. From the printed side of the pattern, stitch on the line between areas #1 and #2. Use a short stitch length and stitch a few stitches beyond the ends of the line.

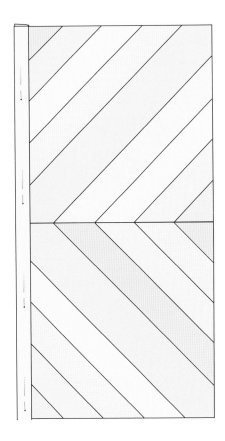

10

5. With the block printed side up, turn the pattern back on the stitching line and trim the seam allowances to ¼" (6 mm).

6. Fold the pattern back in place. Turn the second fabric over area #2; pin.

7. Apply a fabric strip to area #3, following steps 3 to 6. Continue until all the areas have been applied, using one strip of each of the six colors and adding them in random order. Finish the corners with one red and one blue triangle.

8. String-piece all the blocks, adding colors in different arrangements, but always starting with green in the center and ending with red and blue triangles. No two blocks will be the same. Press the blocks. Trim away the excess fabric, leaving a ¼" (6 mm) seam allowance beyond the outer pattern line. Carefully tear away the paper pattern.

9. Arrange the blocks in a pleasing order. The blocks will form a diagonal pattern with alternating red and blue squares at the centers. Sew the blocks together in rows; press the seam allowances open. Then sew the rows together; press the seam allowances open.

10. Measure the pieced quilt; it should be a 28½" (72.3 cm) square. Cut yellow strips to this length. Press the strips in half lengthwise, wrong sides together. Pin them to the sides of the quilt.

11. Sew a red border strip to a blue border strip; press the seam allowances toward the blue. Repeat with the remaining strips to make four sets. Cut the sets to the same length as the yellow strips.

12. Sew a red-blue border set to the top, catching the raw edges of the yellow strip in the seam. Press the seam allowances toward the red. Repeat at the bottom of the quilt. The folded edge of the yellow strip is not stitched down.

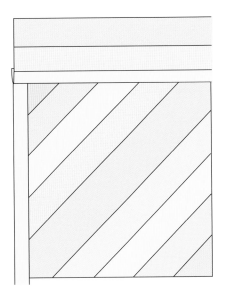

12

13. From the extra pieces of red and blue, cut eight 3" (7.5 cm) sets. Sew these sets into four four-patch squares. Sew the pieced squares to the ends of the remaining pieced borders, alternating colors. Sew these borders to the quilt sides; press the seam allowances toward the borders.

14. Center a green border strip on one side of the quilt. Stitch, beginning and ending ¼" (6 mm) from each corner. Press the seam allowances toward the green. Repeat on each side of the quilt.

15. Fold the quilt top in half diagonally so the border strips overlap at the ends; pin. Mark a line from the point where you stopped stitching to the outer edge of the border. Stitch on the line. Trim the seam allowances to ¼" (6 mm) and press them open. Repeat at each corner to form miters.

16. Cut batting and backing slightly larger than the quilt top. Layer the backing, batting, and quilt top; baste with safety pins or by hand.

17. Thread the top and bobbin of your sewing machine with variegated thread. Quilt by sewing a decorative stitch over the seams of the blocks. Then stitch in the ditch of the border seams.

18. Bind the quilt, following steps 15 to 18 on page 28.

Designer's Tip

Decorative machine stitches used for quilting give your project extra color and texture. I used a feather stitch to quilt and stitched on every other line. Even if you have a machine that only has utility stitches, such as stretch stitches, multi-stitch zigzag, blanket stitch, and hemming stitches, some of them may be suitable for quilting. Experiment with the stitches on your machine to see what you like.

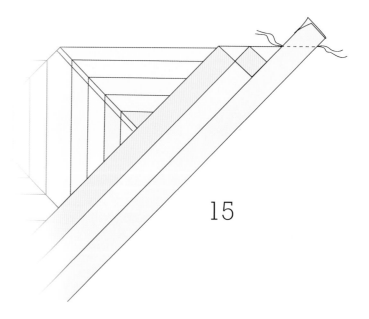

15

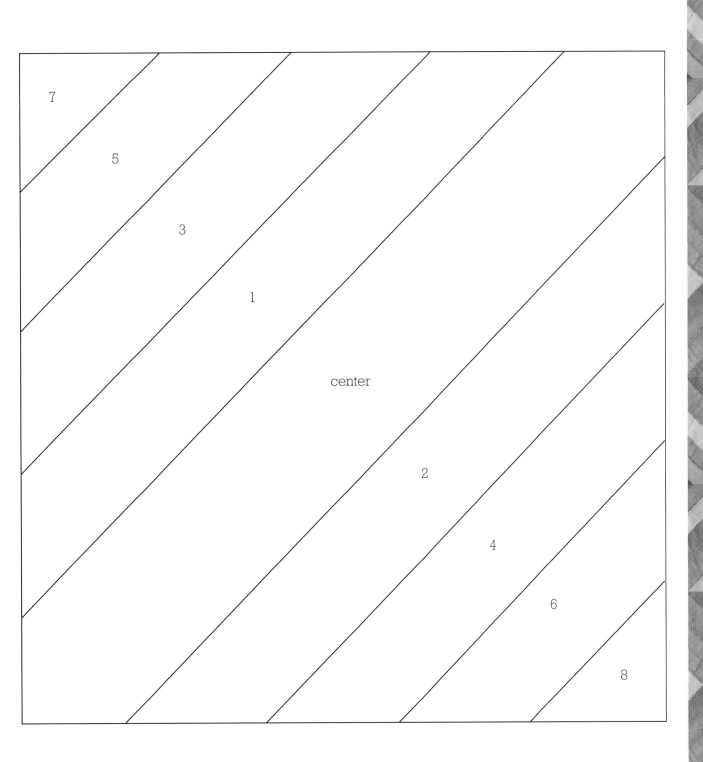

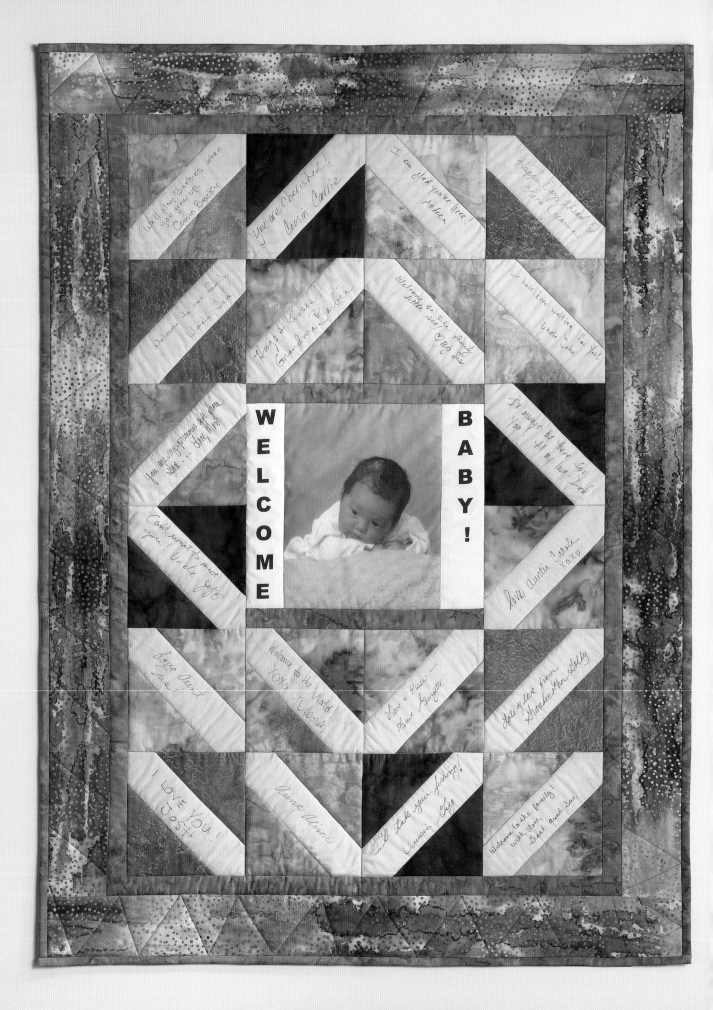

Welcome Baby!

Signature quilt

make a quilt to celebrate the arrival of the new member of the family! A picture of the cutie, printed on fabric, is the center of attraction in this quilt. Photo transfer sheets that are prepared for an inkjet color printer or inkjet color copier make the process easy and fun. Fabric strips for welcome notes and signatures can be filled in at a baby shower or at the hospital after the baby is born. You can send the pieces through the mail to faraway relatives and friends so they can share in the fun. Add quotes about children, nursery rhymes, or poetry to the signature spaces if you like.

Susan Stein

Finished Size: 32" × 44" (81.5 × 112 cm)

Techniques Used: Photo transfer to fabric, writing on fabric

Materials

- ½ yd. (0.5 m) light colored, plain cotton fabric for signatures
- ¼ yd. (0.25 m) each of five fabrics for blocks
- ¼ yd. (0.25 m) fabric for inner border
- ½ yd. (0.5 m) fabric for outer border
- 1⅓ yd. (1.23 m) fabric for backing
- ⅜ yd. (0.35 m) fabric for binding
- Photograph of the baby
- Inkjet printer or copier
- Photo transfer fabric sheets (available at quilt stores)
- Template pattern
- Glue
- Firm cardboard
- Freezer paper
- Permanent marker for writing on fabric
- One low-loft crib batting

Designer's Tip

Iron the signature fabric shapes to freezer paper after you cut them out so the pieces will be easy to sign with a permanent marker. Be sure the signers leave a ¼" (6 mm) margin around the edges for the seam allowances. If you want to make the quilt first and then let people sign it, use a flat cotton batting.

Cutting Directions

Two 1½" × 12½" (3.8 × 31.8 cm) strips of inner border fabric for center panel

Two 1½" × 36½" (3.8 × 91.8 cm) and two 1½" × 26½" (3.8 × 67.3 cm) strips of inner border fabric

Five 2⅝" (6.8 cm) full crosswise strips of signature fabric

Four 5" (12.7 cm) squares from each block fabric; cut each in half diagonally to yield eight triangles

Two 3½" × 38½" (9 × 97.8 cm) strips and two 3½" × 32½" (9 × 82.8 cm) strips of outer border fabric

Four 2½" (6.5 cm) full crosswise strips of binding fabric

1. Enlarge the photo to 8" × 10" (20.5 × 25.5 cm) on the computer or copier. Set the printer for best quality. Run a paper test sheet to make sure the picture will print as expected. Print the photo onto the transfer sheet and allow it to dry, following the manufacturer's directions.

2. Peel off the backing paper in the direction of the grain, not diagonally. Wash the transfer, if necessary, following the manufacturer's directions. Keep the transfer sheet flat so the ink does not smear. Press the sheet when dry.

3. Using a size 72 font on the computer, type WELCOME BABY! vertically in two columns, leaving plenty of space between the words. If you have a horizontal photo, type the words horizontally to be sewn to the top and bottom of the photo. Print WELCOME BABY! onto a photo transfer sheet. Peel and wash as in step 2, above.

4. Cut the photo transfer to 8½" × 10½" (21.8 × 26.7 cm). Cut the WELCOME BABY! strips to 2½" × 10½" (6.5 × 26.7 cm). Sew the strips to the sides of the photo. (If the picture is horizontal, sew the word strips to the top and bottom.)

5. Sew the narrow inner border strips to the top and bottom of the photo panel. Press. The panel should measure 12½" (31.8 cm) square, including the outer seam allowances.

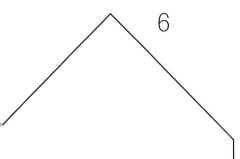

6

6. Trace and glue the template pattern (left) to a piece of firm cardboard and cut out carefully. Use the template to cut a total of 20 pieces from the signature fabric strips.

7. Finger-crease a mark in the center of each side of each signature piece and the diagonal edge of each triangle. Sew matching triangles on each side of the signature pieces, aligning centers. Press the seam allowances toward the triangles. Trim the blocks to an exact 6½" (16.3 cm) square.

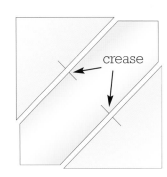

crease

7

8. Arrange the blocks and center panel on a design wall or work surface, balancing colors and following the photograph on page 42.

9. Sew the top row of blocks together; press all the seam allowances in one direction. Repeat for the second row, pressing the seam allowances in the opposite direction. Sew the two rows together, aligning seams.

10. Sew the pairs of blocks on the sides of the center panel together, and then sew them to the center panel. Press the seam allowances away from the center panel.

11. Sew the bottom two rows of blocks together as in step 9. Sew the three units together, aligning seams, and press.

12. Sew the longer inner border strips to the sides of the quilt top. Press the seam allowances toward the borders. Sew the shorter inner border strips to the top and bottom. Repeat for the outer borders. Press the seam allowances toward the borders.

13. Cut batting and backing slightly larger than the quilt top. Layer the backing, batting, and quilt top; baste with safety pins or by hand.

14. Quilt by stitching in the ditch of the seams. Quilt random zigzag lines in the outer border.

15. Bind the quilt as desired.

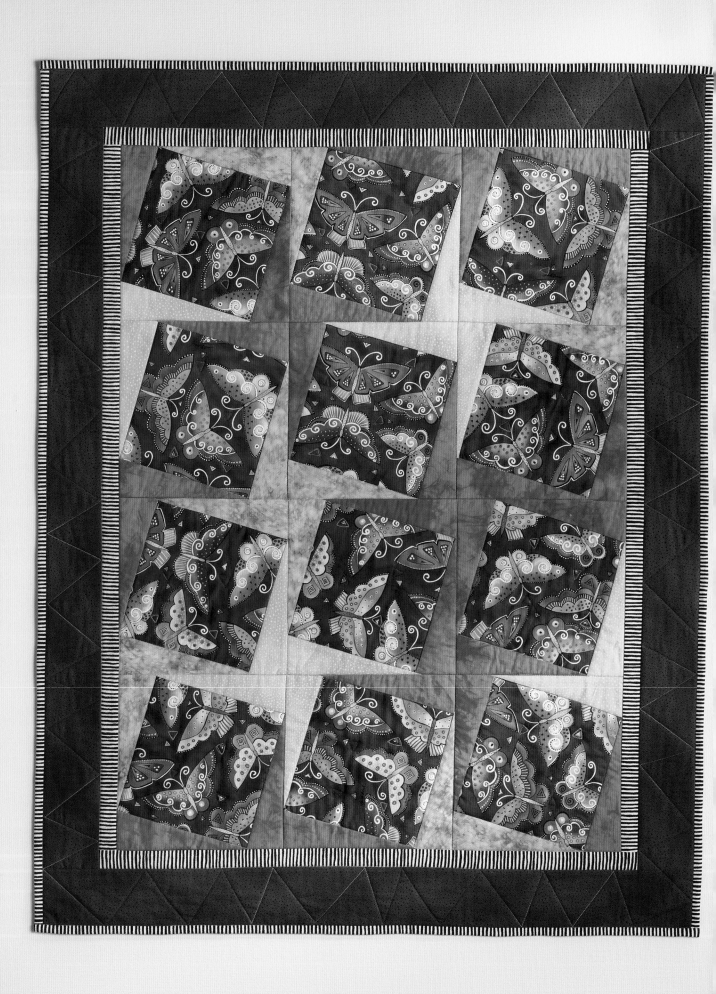

Magic Stars

Contemporary pieced quilt

This lively baby quilt looks complicated but is really easy to make. Choose a brightly patterned fabric for the featured squares and then pick four star fabrics and borders in colors found in the print. The four-pointed stars appear when you put the blocks together. Just lay out the pieces before you sew to keep the colors in order.

Susan Stein

Finished Size: 35" × 44" (89 × 112 cm)

Techniques Used: Contemporary piecing, quilting with variegated thread

Cutting Directions

Twelve 7¾" (20 cm) squares of feature fabric

Five strips 2¾" (7 cm) wide and about 8½" (21.8 cm) long from each star fabric

Four 1½" (3.8 cm) full crosswise strips of inner border fabric

Four 3½" (9 cm) full crosswise strips of outer border fabric

Four 2½" (6.5 cm) full crosswise strips of binding fabric

Materials

- ◼ 1 yd. (0.92 m) feature fabric
- ◼ ⅓ yd. (0.32 m) each of four fabrics for stars
- ◼ ¼ yd. (0.25 m) fabric for inner border
- ◼ ½ yd. (0.5 m) fabric for outer border
- ◼ ½ yd. (0.5 m) fabric for binding
- ◼ 1⅓ yd. (1.23 m) fabric for backing
- ◼ See-through template plastic
- ◼ Permanent black marker
- ◼ Quilter's ruler
- ◼ Rotary cutter and cutting mat
- ◼ One low-loft crib batting
- ◼ Variegated thread

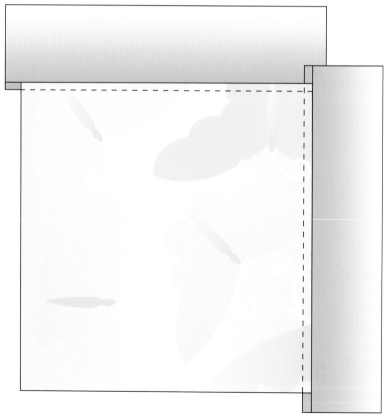

1. Sew a strip of star fabric to a feature fabric square. Turn the seam allowances away from the square.

2. Sew a second strip of star fabric (keeping your colors in order) to the second side of the square, extending the strip about ½" (1.3 cm) beyond each edge of the square. At one end, the second strip overlaps the first strip. Turn the seam allowances away from the square.

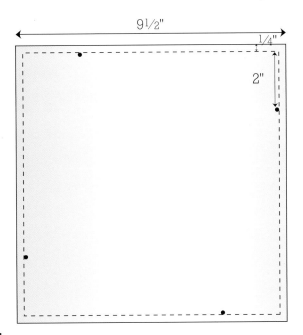

3. Sew the third and fourth strips to the square in the same way, always keeping the seam allowances turned away from the center square.

4. Repeat steps 1 to 3 for the remaining 11 blocks, keeping your colors in the order you planned. Press the blocks carefully.

5. Make a template for trimming the blocks by drawing a 9½" (24.3 cm) square on the plastic with the marker. Draw a second line ¼" (6 mm) inside of the first line to indicate seam allowances. On the inner line, mark a dot 2" (5 cm) from the left-hand corner on each side. Cut out the square on the outside line.

6. Lay the template on the block, with the dots at the corners of the center square. Use the marker to draw around the template.

7. Lay the ruler on the lines and use a rotary cutter to trim off the excess fabric around the block. The block should measure 9½" (24.3 cm).

8. Repeat steps 6 and 7 for the remaining 11 blocks.

9. Sew the blocks together into rows. Sew the rows together, aligning the seams. Press the quilt top thoroughly.

10. Measure the quilt top to bottom through the center. Cut two inner border strips to this length. Sew the inner borders to the sides of the quilt. Press the seam allowances toward the borders.

11. Measure the quilt side to side through the center, including the side borders. Cut two inner border strips to this length. Sew the inner borders to the top and bottom of the quilt. Press the seam allowances toward the borders.

12. Attach the outer border, following the procedure in steps 10 and 11.

13. Cut batting and backing slightly larger than the quilt top. Layer the backing, batting, and quilt top; baste with safety pins or by hand.

14. Thread the top and bobbin of your sewing machine with variegated thread. Quilt by stitching in the ditch of all the seams. Quilt random zigzag lines in the outer border and several small triangles in each feature square.

15. Bind the quilt, beginning with the sides and then the top and bottom.

Designer's Tip

Wash or rinse your fabrics in warm water and machine dry. This will prevent shifting of the grain, bleeding of excess dyes, and puckering when the quilt is laundered later. If possible, preshrink the batting also. Press the fabrics thoroughly before cutting to ensure a crisp look and accurate cutting.

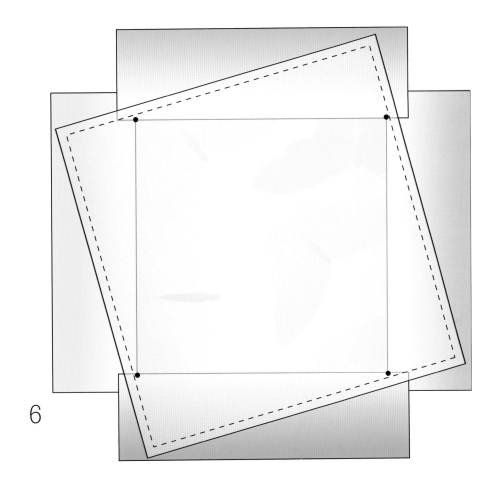

6

Puzzle Blocks

Triangle squares quilt

*L*ook at all the fun you can have with triangle squares. This project is like a sampler quilt showing six different ways of arranging the same number of triangle squares to create a totally different look in each block. Each block also uses different color combinations, yet they are all tied together with a happy print border.

Susan Stein

FINISHED SIZE: 38" × 52" (96.5 × 132 cm)

TECHNIQUES USED: Grid-pieced triangle squares, quilting with variegated thread

Materials

- ¼ yd. (0.25 m) each of three light or warm colored fabrics
- ¼ yd. (0.25 m) each of three darker or cool colored fabrics
- ⅝ yd. (0.6 m) fabric for sashing
- ¾ yd. (0.7 m) fabric for border
- 1⅝ yd. (1.5 m) fabric for backing
- ½ yd. (0.5 m) fabric for binding
- Foundation-piecing paper
- One low-loft crib batting
- Variegated thread

Cutting Directions

Four 9" (23 cm) squares from each of the light and dark fabrics

Seven 2½" (6.5 cm) full crosswise strips of the sashing fabric; from three of the strips, cut nine 12½" (31.8 cm) strips; cut the remaining four strips 30½" (77.3 cm) long

Four 4½" (11.5 cm) full crosswise strips of border fabric

Five 2½" (6.5 cm) full crosswise strips of binding fabric; piece the side binding strips with diagonal seams

4

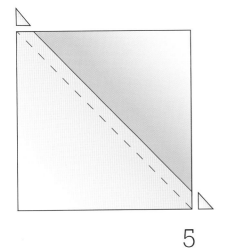

5

Designer's Tip

The seam of the triangle-square is on the bias, so take care when pressing it so it doesn't stretch and ripple. Rather than sliding the iron down the length of the seam, turn the seam allowances to one side and press them in place, moving the iron in the direction of the grain lines.

1. Match up two different squares of block fabric—one light and one dark, or one cool and one warm—for a total of 12 combinations. You will have to repeat some. Place the pairs of fabrics right sides together.

2. Make 12 copies of the stitching guide on page 56. If you draw them by hand, begin with a 7¾" (20 cm) square. If you copy them using a copy machine, make sure the size is not distorted. Pin one sheet of the stitching guide to each pair of block fabrics, using two pins in the center and a pin at each corner.

3. Sew on all of the dashed lines of the stitching guide, using a short stitch length. If your stitch length is too long, it will be difficult to remove the paper after sewing.

4. Cut on all of the solid lines of the stitching guide, through all of the layers. Carefully tear away the paper pattern from the triangles.

5. Press the triangle-squares with the seam allowances to one side. Trim off the "dog ears." Keep the colors sorted into stacks.

6. Create six stacks of two color combinations each. One color should be present in both combinations.

7. Sew the triangle-squares together into blocks arranged in different ways, as shown in the photo on page 52. Press.

8. Arrange the blocks on a design wall or work surface, balancing colors.

9. Sew short sashing strips between each pair of blocks and at the ends of the rows. Press the seam allowances toward the sashing.

10. Sew the long sashing strips between the rows of blocks and at the top and bottom of the quilt. Make sure the blocks align vertically.

11. Measure the quilt top to bottom through the center. Cut two border strips to this length. Sew the borders to the sides of the quilt. Press the seam allowances toward the borders.

12. Measure the quilt side to side through the center, including the side borders. Cut two border strips to this length. Sew the borders to the top and bottom of the quilt. Press the seam allowances toward the borders.

13. Cut batting and backing slightly larger than the quilt top. Layer the backing, batting, and quilt top; baste with safety pins or by hand.

14. Thread the top and bobbin of your sewing machine with variegated thread. Quilt by stitching in the ditch of all the sashing seams and around each block. Quilt each block in a pattern that suits the arrangement of the triangle-squares. Stitch crisscrossing wavy lines in the border.

15. Bind the quilt, beginning with the sides and then the top and bottom.

Bonnets and Booties

Appliquéd silhouettes quilt

imple shapes of baby accessories make a bold statement on this monochromatic quilt. Bias tapes in a matching color highlight the appliqués and make for a very quick binding on the scalloped borders. Choose light and dark pinks for a girl, or go with any light and dark color combo to blend with your nursery décor.

Janis Bullis

FINISHED SIZE: 36" × 44½" (91.5 × 113.3 cm)

TECHNIQUES USED: Satin-stitch appliqué, scalloped edge, binding with bias tape

Cutting Directions

One 36" × 44½" (91.5 × 113.3 cm) light blue rectangle for quilt top

One 7" (18 cm) dark blue square for buggy appliqué

Four 7" × 3" (18 × 7.5 cm) dark blue rectangles for bottle appliqués

Four 4" (10 cm) dark blue squares for pacifier appliqués

Twelve 6" (15 cm) dark blue squares for bonnet and bootie appliqués

Fusible web pieces in the same sizes as all the appliqué pieces

Materials

- 1¾ yd. (1.6 m) dark blue fabric for backing and appliqués
- 1⅜ yd. (1.3 m) light blue fabric
- ¾ yd. (0.7 m) paper-backed fusible adhesive web, 20" (51 cm) wide
- Tracing paper
- 6¼ yd. (5.75 m) extra wide double-fold bias tape, ½" (1.3 cm) wide
- Tear-away stabilizer
- 3 yd. (2.75 m) single-fold bias tape, ½" (1.3 cm) wide
- One low-loft crib batting
- Dark blue thread

1. Fuse an adhesive web piece to the wrong side of each appliqué piece. Do not remove the protective paper backing yet.

2. Trace the appliqué patterns on pages 64 to 65 and cut them out. Trace each appliqué pattern onto the paper backing of the fusible web. Note that the appliqués will appear in the opposite direction from the pattern. For some shapes, you will need to trace half of them in one direction and then flip the pattern over to trace the others. Cut out the appliqués.

3. Mark lines lengthwise, crosswise, and diagonally across the center of the quilt top. Mark a line 1" (2.5 cm) from the outer edge.

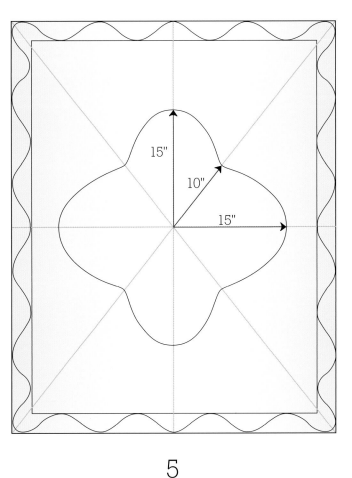

15"

10"

15"

5

4. Trace and cut out the scallop templates on page 63; note that one is for the sides and one is for the top and bottom. Align the center point on the template to the center of one side of the quilt top, with the guideline on the template on the marked line 1" (2.5 cm) from the fabric edge. Mark the scalloped edge, repositioning the template until you are about 2¼" (6 cm) from the corners. Repeat for the other side and for the top and bottom. Round the four corners to join the lines.

5. Draw a pattern for the inner frame on paper, following the diagram. Fold the pattern in half lengthwise and crosswise to check for symmetry and to mark centerlines. Center the pattern on the quilt top and trace around it.

6. Arrange the appliqués on the quilt top as in the photograph on page 58. Remove the paper backing from the appliqués and fuse them to the quilt top, following the manufacturer's directions.

7. Cut 23" (58.5 cm) of extra wide double-fold bias tape, and press it in half lengthwise. Cut it into nine 2½" (6.5 cm) pieces. Topstitch the pieces to the quilt top to make two ties for each bonnet and a curved buggy handle.

8. Satin stitch the edges of all the appliqués, using matching thread. Use tear-away stabilizer under the fabric to support the stitches and prevent puckering. Tear the stabilizer away.

9. Press the quilt top. Cut batting and backing slightly larger than the quilt top. Layer the backing, batting, and quilt top; baste with safety pins or by hand. Machine-baste ¼" (6 mm) from the marked scallop line.

10. Pin or hand-baste the single-fold bias tape over the marked line for the inner frame, pinning though all the layers. Stitch the bias tape in place along both edges.

11. Stitch close to the outer edge of the buggy through all layers of the quilt.

12. Trim along the scallop lines through all layers of the quilt. Unfold the extra wide double-fold bias tape and pin it to the outer edge of the quilt, right sides together. Stitch in the crease of the first fold, $\frac{1}{2}$" (1.3 cm) from the quilt edge.

13. Wrap the bias tape over the quilt edge to the wrong side, and pin in place. Hand-stitch the tape to the wrong side of the quilt along the fold.

Designer's Tip

The stitching around the inner frame and the buggy will hold the quilt layers together. If you want to add more quilting stitches, you can outline some of the other appliqués.

top/bottom scallop template

side scallop template

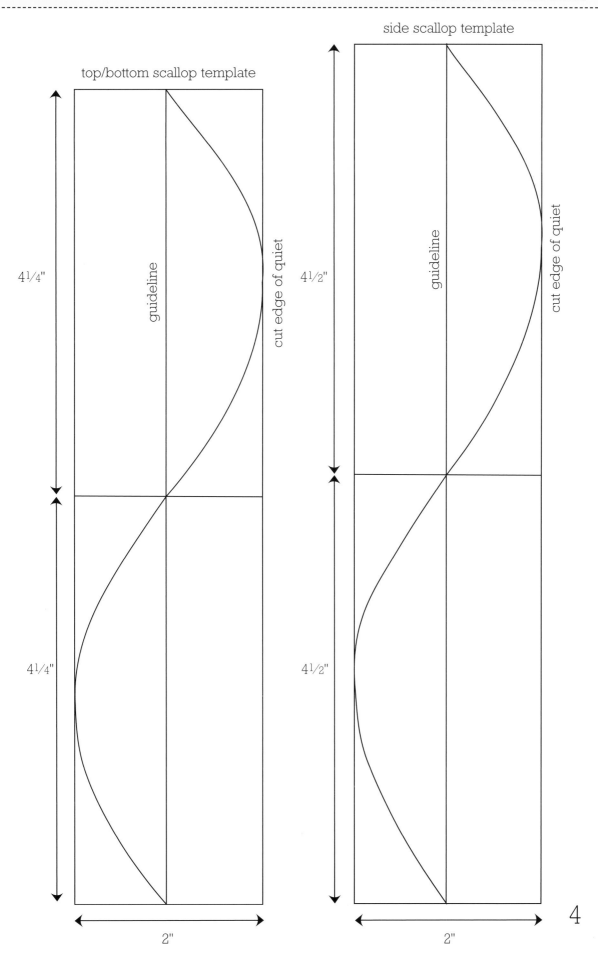

guideline

cut edge of quiet

guideline

cut edge of quiet

4¼"

4¼"

4½"

4½"

2"

2"

4

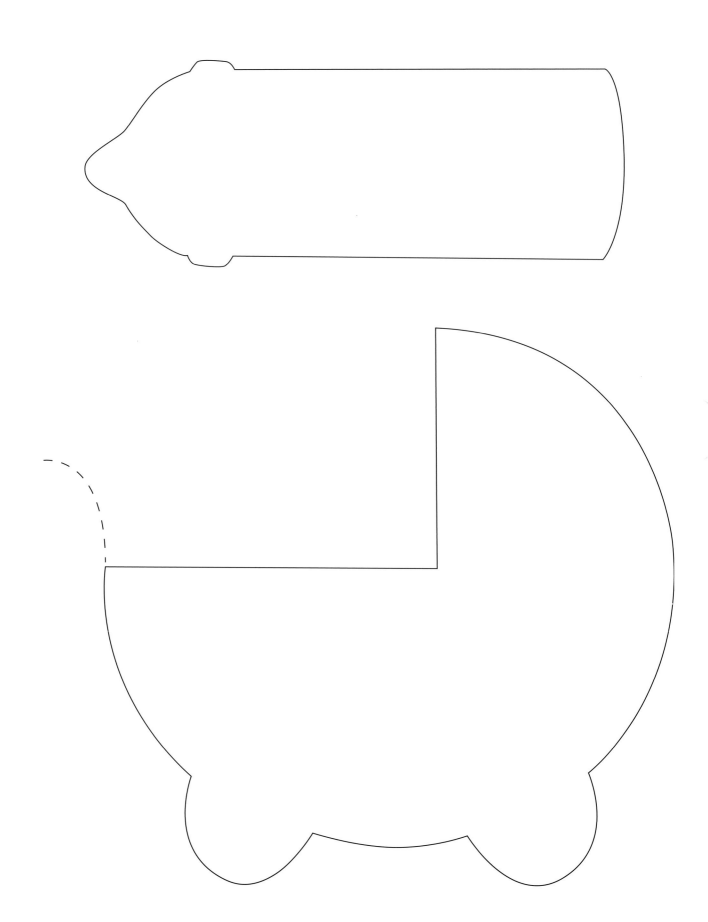

Bugs by the Dozen

Appliquéd block quilt

Crawly critters and fluttery fellows are fun and easy appliqués on a quilt designed for a baby or toddler. Choose pastel prints for the background blocks and small brightly colored prints for the appliqués. Bright colors for the sashing, borders, and binding help frame the blocks.

Janis Bullis

FINISHED SIZE: 31" × 40½" (78.5 × 103 cm)

TECHNIQUES USED: Satin-stitch appliqué

Cutting Directions

One 8½" (21.8 cm) square of each of the block fabrics

One 8" (20.5 cm) square of each of the appliqué fabrics

Twelve 8" (20.5 cm) squares of fusible web

Eight 2" (5 cm) strips of sashing/border fabric; cut nine 8½" (21.8 cm) sashing strips from two strips

Four 2½" (6.5 cm) binding strips

Materials

- ¼ yd. (0.25 m) each of 12 solid-color fabrics for blocks
- ¼ yd. (0.25 m) each of 12 mini-print fabrics for appliqués
- ½ yd. (0.5 m) fabric for sashing and border
- 1¼ yd. (1.15 m) fabric for quilt backing
- 1¼ yd. (1.15 m) fabric for binding
- 1⅜ yd. (1.3 m) paper-backed fusible adhesive web, 20" (51 cm) wide
- Tracing paper
- Tear-away stabilizer
- One low-loft crib batting
- Thread to match each appliqué color

1. Fuse an adhesive web square to the wrong side of each appliqué square. Do not remove the protective paper backing yet.

2. Enlarge the appliqué patterns on pages 70 to 73 and cut them out. Trace each appliqué pattern onto the paper backing of the fusible web. Note that the appliqués will appear in the opposite direction from the pattern. Cut out the appliqués.

3. Remove the paper backing from each appliqué and fuse it to a quilt block, following the manufacturer's directions.

4. Satin stitch the edges of all the appliqués, using matching thread. Use tear-away stabilizer under the fabric to support the stitches and prevent puckering. Use a narrow satin stitch for antennae and feet. Tear the stabilizer away.

5. Arrange the blocks on a design wall or work surface. Sew each column of blocks together with short sashing strips between them. Press the seam allowances toward the sashing.

6. Measure all the columns. Cut two sashing strips and two borders to the length of the shortest column. Sew the columns together with sashing strips between them. Make sure the blocks align horizontally. Sew the borders to the sides. Press all the seam allowances toward the sashing and borders.

7. Measure the quilt side to side through the center, including the side borders. Cut two border strips to this length. Sew the borders to the top and bottom of the quilt.

8. Press the quilt top. Cut batting and backing slightly larger than the quilt top. Layer the backing, batting, and quilt top; baste with safety pins or by hand.

9. Quilt ¼" (6 mm) inside the seam of each block.

10. Bind the quilt as desired.

Designer's Tip

Practice satin stitching on a sharp curve. To keep the stitches perpendicular to the edge as you round a corner, stop with the needle down in the fabric on the outside stitch, lift the presser foot, turn the fabric slightly, lower the presser foot, and continue. Pivot like this as often as necessary to suit the sharpness of the curve.

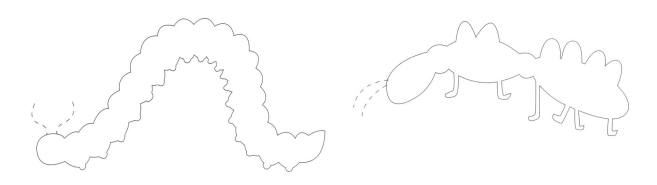

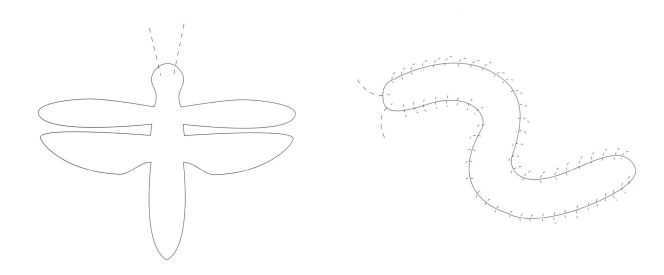

HALF SCALE: ENLARGE 200% ON COPIER

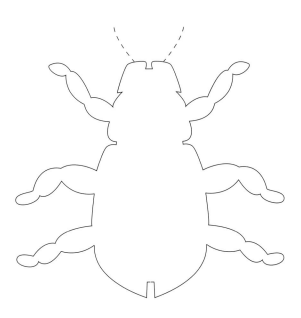

Half scale: Enlarge 200% on copier

HALF SCALE: ENLARGE 200% ON COPIER

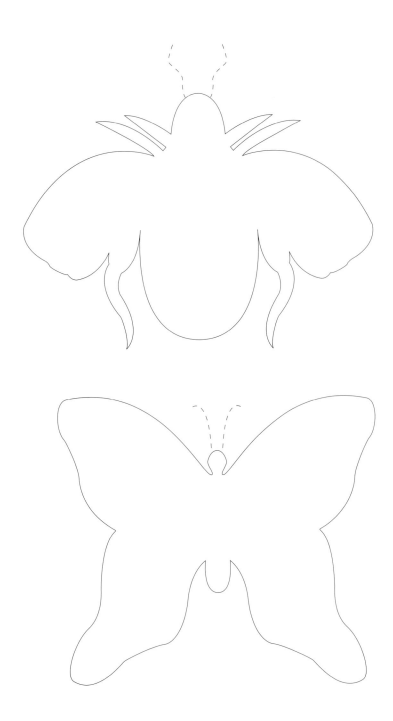

HALF SCALE: ENLARGE 200% ON COPIER

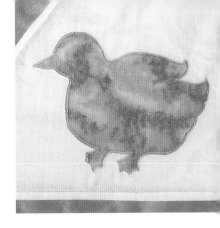

Fuzzy Friends

Appliquéd medallion quilt

Made from soft and cuddly flannel fabrics, this baby quilt is perfect for the crib or as a take-along blanket. Appliqués of furry animals surround an extra-large teddy bear. Wide bias binding gives this flannel quilt a soft edge and acts as another border to frame the quilt top.

Janis Bullis

FINISHED SIZE: 32" × 40" (81.5 × 102 cm)

TECHNIQUES USED: Satin-stitch appliqué, wide bias binding

Cutting Directions

One 13½" × 17½" (34.3 × 44.3 cm) rectangle of yellow and lavender flannel; cut each in half diagonally

One 26" × 33" (66 × 84 cm) diamond (see step 1) of pink flannel

One 18" × 20" (46 × 51 cm) square of blue flannel for appliqué

Two 8" (20.5 cm) squares of green flannel for appliqués

Three 8" (20.5 cm) squares of hot pink flannel for appliqués

Fusible web pieces the same sizes as the appliqué pieces

Eight 2½" (6.5 cm) full crosswise strips of purple flannel; cut two strips 40" (102 cm) long for side borders; cut two strips 32" (81.5 cm) long for top and bottom borders; cut four strips 48" (122 cm) long for sashing

Bias strips 4" (10 cm) wide, joined to a length of about 4¼ yd. (3.9 m) (See step 14)

Materials

- 1 yd. (0.92 m) pink flannel for center diamond
- ½ yd. (0.5 m) each of yellow and lavender flannel for corner triangles
- ½ yd. (0.5 m) blue flannel for bear appliqué
- ¼ yd. (0.25 m) green flannel for cat and duck appliqués
- 1 yd. (0.92 m) hot pink flannel for sheep, bunny, bow, and binding
- 1½ yd. (1.4 m) purple flannel for sashing and borders
- 1¼ yd. (1.15 m) flannel for quilt backing
- ⅞ yd. (0.8 m) paper-backed fusible adhesive web, 20" (51 cm) wide
- Tracing paper
- Tear-away stabilizer
- Thread to match appliqué colors
- One low-loft crib batting

1. Fold the pink flannel in half lengthwise and crosswise. Mark points from the folded corner 16½" (41.8 cm) on the lengthwise fold and 13" (33 cm) on the crosswise fold. Draw a straight line connecting the marks. Cut on the line to form the center diamond.

2. Fuse an adhesive web square to the wrong side of each appliqué fabric square. Do not remove the protective paper backing yet.

3. Enlarge the appliqué patterns on pages 78 to 81 and cut them out. Trace each appliqué onto the paper backing of the fusible web. Note that the appliqués will appear in the opposite direction from the pattern. Cut out the appliqués.

4. Remove the paper backing from each appliqué and fuse it to its flannel background piece, following the manufacturer's directions. Don't fuse the bow to the teddy bear yet.

Designer's Tip

The diamond shape may have become distorted while you were stitching the appliqué. Draw a paper diamond to the same dimensions and use it as a guide for the length of the sashing strips.

5. Satin stitch the edges of all the appliqués, using matching thread. Use tear-away stabilizer under the fabric to support the stitches and prevent puckering. After stitching the teddy bear, fuse and stitch the bow in place. Tear the stabilizer away.

6. Stitch a sashing strip to one side of the diamond, taking care not to stretch the side of the diamond. Align the strip to a diamond point at one end and allow the strip to extend beyond the other end. Press the seam allowances away from the diamond.

7. Repeat step 6 for the other three sides, working your way around the diamond. Each strip will overlap the previous sashing strip. Trim away excess fabric after all the pieces are sewn in place.

8. Sew the triangles to the outer edges of the sashing strips. Press the seam allowances toward the sashing.

9. Center a border strip on one side of the quilt. Stitch, beginning and ending ¼" (6 mm) from the corners. Press the seam allowances toward the border. Repeat on each side of the quilt.

10. Fold the quilt top in half diagonally, right sides together, so the border strips overlap at the ends; pin. Mark a line from the point where you stopped stitching to the outer edge of the border. Stitch on the line. Trim the seam allowances to ¼" (6 mm) and press them open. Repeat at each corner to form miters. See the illustration on page 40.

11. Cut batting and backing slightly larger than the quilt top. Layer the backing, batting, and quilt top; baste with safety pins or by hand.

12. Outline-quilt the triangles and diamond. Add any other quilting stitches you want.

13. Trim the batting and backing layer even with the quilt top. Stitch ¼" (6 mm) from the edges.

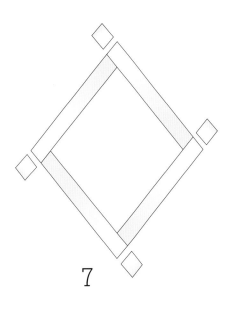

7

14. Stitch the bias binding strips together with diagonal seams; press the seam allowances open. Stitch the binding to the right side of the quilt edge, using a 1" (2.5 cm) seam allowance and beginning at the middle of the lower edge.

15. To miter corners, stitch to within 1" (2.5 cm) of the corner. Turn the binding to align the cut edge with the adjacent side, creating a hidden diagonal fold underneath and a visible fold aligned with the lower edge of the quilt. Pin and stitch the adjacent side 1" (2.5 cm) from the cut edge. Repeat at all the corners.

16. Before completing the stitching, join the ends of the binding with a diagonal seam.

17. Wrap the folded edge of the strip to the wrong side of the quilt. Turn under the edge 1" (2.5 cm) and pin in place. Hand-stitch the fold to the back of the quilt.

15

HALF SCALE: ENLARGE 200% ON COPIER

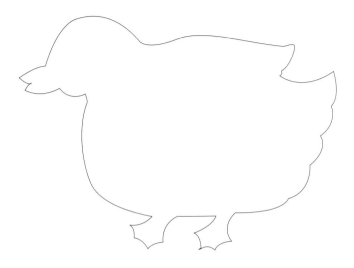

HALF SCALE: ENLARGE 200% ON COPIER

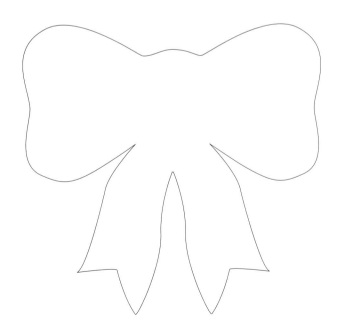

HALF SCALE: ENLARGE 200% ON COPIER

HALF SCALE: ENLARGE 200% ON COPIER

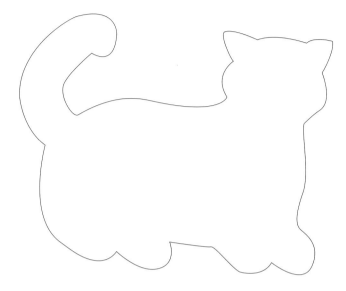

HALF SCALE: ENLARGE 200% ON COPIER

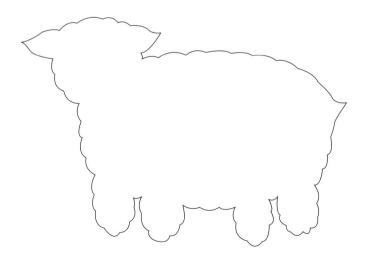

HALF SCALE: ENLARGE 200% ON COPIER

Christening Quilt

Embellished whole-cloth quilt

*Y*ou can create a family heirloom quilt without hours of detailed stitching or handwork. This project takes advantage of fancy fabrics, like cotton eyelet and polyester satin, and is embellished with ready-made Battenberg and cutwork hearts. Decorative stitches on your sewing machine, sewn in irregular diagonal lines, create the look of an old-fashioned crazy quilt in far less time.

Phyllis Dobbs

FINISHED SIZE: 40½" × 56" (103 × 142 cm)

TECHNIQUES USED: Whole-cloth quilting, machine embroidery stitches, straight-stitch appliqué

Cutting Directions

One 32½" × 48½" (82.8 × 123.3 cm) eyelet panel

One 32½" × 48½" (82.8 × 123.3 cm) satin panel

Two 5" × 48½" (12.7 × 123.3 cm) strips of satin for side borders

Two 5" × 40½" (12.7 × 103 cm) strips of satin for top and bottom borders

Four or five 2½" (6.5 cm) full crosswise strips of eyelet for binding

Materials

- 3½ yd. (3.2 m) white satin fabric for lining, backing, and borders
- 1⅔ yd. (1.58 m) white eyelet fabric for outer layer and binding
- One low-loft crib batting
- Temporary spray adhesive for fabric
- Two spools #40 white rayon thread
- 12 to 15 assorted Battenberg and cutwork hearts, 2" to 4" (5 to 10 cm) wide
- White pearl beads
- 18 yd. (16.56 m) white satin ribbon, ⅛" (3 mm) wide
- Sewing machine with built-in decorative stitches

Designer's Tip

Temporary fabric adhesive in a convenient spray can holds the quilt top, batting, and backing layers together for quilting. This is especially useful when you are working with slippery fabrics like satin. It won't gum up your needle while you sew. For some brands, the adhesive simply diminishes after a few weeks. For others it can be removed by laundering. Check the label and follow the manufacturer's directions.

5

1. Smooth the satin panel, right side up, on the work surface. Spray it lightly with temporary spray adhesive. Smooth the eyelet panel, right side up, over the satin. Pin the edges as necessary.

2. Sew the side borders to the center panel. Press the seam allowances toward the borders.

3. Sew the top and bottom borders to the quilt top. Press the seam allowances toward the borders.

4. Cut batting and backing slightly larger than the quilt top. Layer the backing, batting, and quilt top, applying spray adhesive lightly between layers. Also baste with a few safety pins.

5. Thread the machine with rayon thread. Using various machine embroidery stitches, quilt the center panel in lines resembling a crazy quilt.

6. Quilt the borders with a large, freeform pattern.

7. Arrange Battenberg and cutwork hearts on the center panel. Pin them in place or secure them temporarily with spray adhesive. Straight stitch near the outer edge of each heart.

8. Hand-stitch a pearl bead at the top center of each heart.

9. Cut seven 2-yd. (1.85 m) lengths of ribbon and seven ½-yd. (0.5 m) lengths of ribbon. Fold a long ribbon into a bow with five or six loops on each side, leaving long tails. Tie the center of the loops with a shorter ribbon. Repeat to make seven bows. Stitch a bow at each corner of the center panel. Stitch the other three bows at random places on the center panel.

10. Trim the edges of the quilt even with the quilt top. Bind the quilt as desired.

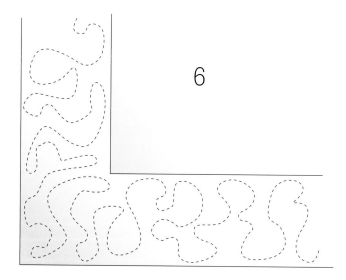

6

9

Pictures in the Clouds

Quilted shapes on big blocks

Design motifs in pretty quilt fabrics can be adapted for quilting templates. Here I drew simple shapes that resemble details from the print blocks and used them to quilt in the white blocks. White quilting thread on white fabric makes the designs very subtle. Once the quilt is washed and the batting shrinks and fluffs up a little, the designs become more apparent.

You can use this idea for brightly colored quilts, too. Use quilting thread that matches the block colors or use variegated thread that ties in all the colors of the quilt.

Phyllis Dobbs

FINISHED SIZE: 33" × 48" (84 × 122 cm)

TECHNIQUES USED: Large block piecing, template quilting

Cutting Directions

Twelve 8½" (21.8 cm) squares of print fabric

Twelve 8½" (21.8 cm) squares of white fabric

Four 2½" (6.5 cm) full crosswise strips of binding; piece together in diagonal seams

Materials

- ¾ yd. (0.7 m) print fabric
- ¾ yd. (0.7 m) white fabric
- 1⅔ yd. (1.58 m) contrast fabric for backing and binding
- Computer and scanner or copy machine
- Air-soluble fabric-marking pen
- One low-loft crib batting

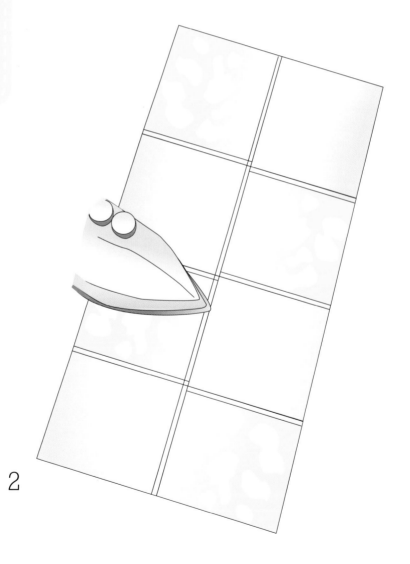

2

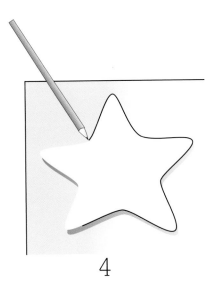

4

1. Sew four blocks together for each of six rows, alternating print and white blocks in each row. Press all the seam allowances toward the print blocks.

2. Sew the rows together, aligning the seams and keeping the seam allowances turned as they were pressed. Press the quilt top.

3. Enlarge and print the fabric motifs to the size you want, using a computer and scanner or a copy machine. Simplify the designs, if necessary, and cut them out to use as quilting templates.

4. Center the quilting templates on the white blocks, and trace around them using air-soluble marking pen.

5. Cut batting and backing slightly larger than the quilt top. Layer the backing, batting, and quilt top; baste with safety pins or by hand.

6. Quilt on the marked lines in the white blocks. Then quilt the print blocks with parallel lines 1" (2.5 cm) apart, alternating the direction of the lines from one block to the next.

7. Bind the quilt as desired.

Designer's Tip

I used air-soluble marking pen because it disappears completely and I knew I would complete the quilting within a few hours. If you set the project aside and don't return to it for a day or two, the marks will be gone. So plan on marking the quilt top just before quilting it.

Baby Animals

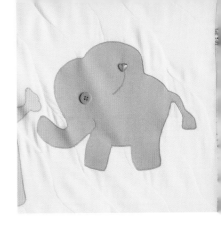

Juvenile print with matching appliqués

*L*ots of cute cotton print fabrics have individual motifs that would make great appliqués if only they were larger. Here is a quick and easy way to use these designs to embellish the center panel of a bordered whole-cloth quilt. All you need is a computer and scanner or a copy machine.

I've used little buttons and beads to accent my baby animal designs in this quilt that will be used as a wall hanging. To make the quilt baby-safe, add these details with fabric paint or embroidery.

Phyllis Dobbs

Finished Size: 40" × 52" (102 × 132 cm)

Techniques Used: Whole-cloth quilting, machine satin-stitch appliqué

Materials

- 2⅔ yd. (2.48 m) print fabric for borders and backing
- 1 yd. (0.92 m) solid pastel fabric
- Pastel fabrics for appliqués
- Computer and scanner or copy machine
- Steam-A-Seam 2 fusible web
- Tear-away stabilizer
- Coordinating thread
- One low-loft cotton crib batting
- Buttons and beads for embellishment (if used as a wall hanging)

Cutting Directions

One 24" × 36" (61 × 91.5 cm) pastel center panel

Four 8½" (21.8 cm) full crosswise strips of border fabric; cut two strips 36" (91.5 cm) long and two strips 40" (102 cm) long

Five 2½" (6.5 cm) full crosswise strips of pastel fabric for binding

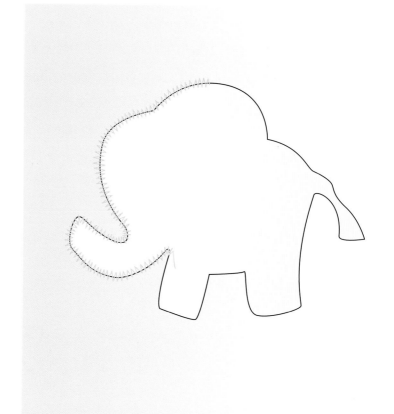

6

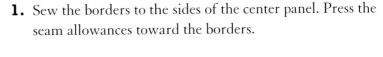

1. Sew the borders to the sides of the center panel. Press the seam allowances toward the borders.

2. Sew the borders to the top and bottom. Press the seam allowances toward the borders.

3. Enlarge and print the fabric motifs to the size you want, using a computer and scanner or a copy machine. Simplify the designs, if necessary, and cut them out.

4. Remove the loose paper from one side of the fusible web. Smooth appliqué fabrics onto the fusible web. Trace the appliqué patterns onto the fabric, and cut them out.

5. Remove the paper backing from the appliqués and smooth them in place on the center panel. When you are pleased with the arrangement, fuse them in place with an iron, following the manufacturer's directions.

6. Place tear-away stabilizer on the back of the center panel, under the appliqués. Satin stitch the edges of the appliqués, using matching thread. Add any detail stitching. Carefully tear away the stabilizer.

7. Press the quilt top. Cut batting and backing slightly larger than the quilt top. Layer the backing, batting, and quilt top; baste with safety pins or by hand.

8. Quilt by machine, stitching wavy diagonal lines about 3" (7.5 cm) apart across the center panel. When you are within ¼" (6 mm) of an appliqué, gradually shorten the stitch length down to 0 and stitch in place to lock the thread. Begin stitching on the other side of the appliqué by stitching in place and then increasing the stitch length to normal to continue the wavy line.

9. Quilt the borders with closer wavy lines that run from the center panel outward; quilt the corners diagonally.

10. Bind the quilt as desired.

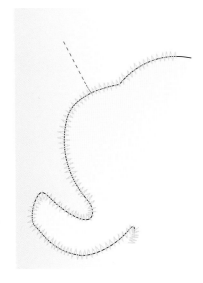

8

Meet the Quilt Designers

■ Janis Bullis

Janis has been serving the home decorating and craft industries for more than twenty years as a consultant and designer. She lives in Central Valley, New York. Her clients include book, magazine, and pattern publishers, as well as craft and textile manufacturers. Janis has contributed as author, editor, and designer to more than 100 how-to publications whose topics range from bridal accouterments and baby accessories to holiday decorating. Her favorite media are fabric and trims.

■ Phyllis Dobbs

Phyllis began stitching at a very early age and was taught needlework, sewing, and quilting by her mother and aunt. She gained a great love and appreciation for quilting from her grandmother's and great-grandmother's quilts, which she safeguards in her home. Phyllis began designing professionally in 1984 and formed her own company, Lucky Duck Designs. She has published over 1,000 needlework and quilt designs. Her design studio, which occupies the second floor of her home in Alabama, is a collage of fabrics, fibers, beads, buttons, and inspirational materials. Her web site is www.phyllisdobbs.com.

■ Sharon Hultgren

Sharon has been working in the quilting industry for close to twenty years. She owned a quilt shop for four years and continues to teach quilting classes across the United States and around the world. Her favorite venue for teaching is the weekend retreat, where quilters can relax and have fun while they learn. Sharon has invented several tools to make quilting easier, including the Easy Angle for accurately cutting triangles,

squares, and other shapes from fabric strips. Recently, Sharon designed a new product called Foundation by the Yard©. These fabric panels, printed with patterns of quilt blocks to be foundation-pieced, are being produced by Benartex Fabrics. Sharon lives in northern Minnesota.

■ Gerri Robinson

Gerri Robinson, from Dublin, Ohio, is a relative newcomer to the quilting scene, having taken her first class in 1998. In the five years that followed, Gerri learned the many different piecing techniques and discovered all the tools that make piecing and quilting easy. Her talent for sewing and design quickly won her commissions for companies like Benartex, Robert Kaufman, King's Road, and Free Spirit. Love for color, fabric, texture, and the freedom to create inspired Gerri to design her own patterns, which she has been publishing under her brand, Planted Seed Designs, since 2004. Her designs have appeared in McCall's Quilting, McCall's Quick Quilts, and Fabric Trends. Check her out at www.plantedseeddesigns.com.

■ Susan Stein

Susan has been quilting since 1977 and has completed several hundred projects for publications, store samples, walls, beds, gifts, commissions, teaching, and lecturing. She owns a successful quilt shop in St. Paul, Minnesota, called Colorful Quilts and Textiles. As an author of two books, Susan frequently focuses on contemporary quilts in collage style, Double Wedding Ring patterns, and sampler-style quilts. In 2003, Susan was voted the Minnesota Quilter of the Year. Check out Susan's store and some of her work at www.colorfulquiltsandtextiles.com.